by Iain Gray

Lang Syne

PUBLISHING

WRITING *to* REMEMBER

Lang**Syne**

PUBLISHING

WRITING *to* REMEMBER

79 Main Street, Newtongrange,
Midlothian EH22 4NA
Tel: 0131 344 0414   Fax: 0845 075 6085
E-mail: info@lang-syne.co.uk
www.langsyneshop.co.uk

Design by Dorothy Meikle
Printed by Ricoh Print Scotland
© Lang Syne Publishers Ltd 2012

ISBN 978-1-85217-416-3

Aitken

MOTTO:

Strength and vigilance.

CREST:

An oak tree.

NAME variations include:
Aiken
Aikens
Aitkens
Aitkin
Atkin
Aitcheson

*The spirit of the clan means
much to thousands of people*

Chapter one:

The origins of the clan system

by Rennie McOwan

The original Scottish clans of the Highlands and the great families of the Lowlands and Borders were gatherings of families, relatives, allies and neighbours for mutual protection against rivals or invaders.

Scotland experienced invasion from the Vikings, the Romans and English armies from the south. The Norman invasion of what is now England also had an influence on land-holding in Scotland. Some of these invaders stayed on and in time became 'Scottish'.

The word clan derives from the Gaelic language term 'clann', meaning children, and it was first used many centuries ago as communities were formed around tribal lands in glens and mountain fastnesses.

The format of clans changed over the centuries, but at its best the chief and his family held the land on behalf of all, like trustees, and the ordinary clansmen and women believed they had a blood relationship with the founder of their clan.

There were two way duties and obligations. An inadequate chief could be deposed and replaced by someone of greater ability.

Clan people had an immense pride in race. Their relationship with the chief was like adult children to a father and they had a real dignity.

The concept of clanship is very old and a more feudal notion of authority gradually crept in.

Pictland, for instance, was divided into seven principalities ruled by feudal leaders who were the strongest and most charismatic leaders of their particular groups.

By the sixth century the 'British' kingdoms of Strathclyde, Lothian and Celtic Dalriada (Argyll) had emerged and Scotland, as one nation, began to take shape in the time of King Kenneth MacAlpin.

Some chiefs claimed descent from ancient kings which may not have been accurate in every case.

By the twelfth and thirteenth centuries the clans and families were more strongly brought under the central control of Scottish monarchs.

Lands were awarded and administered more and more under royal favour, yet the power of the area clan chiefs was still very great.

The long wars to ensure Scotland's

independence against the expansionist ideas of English monarchs extended the influence of some clans and reduced the lands of others.

Those who supported Scotland's greatest king, Robert the Bruce, were awarded the territories of the families who had opposed his claim to the Scottish throne.

In the Scottish Borders country – the notorious Debatable Lands – the great families built up a ferocious reputation for providing warlike men accustomed to raiding into England and occasionally fighting one another.

Chiefs had the power to dispense justice and to confiscate lands and clan warfare produced a society where martial virtues – courage, hardiness, tenacity – were greatly admired.

Gradually the relationship between the clans and the Crown became strained as Scottish monarchs became more orientated to life in the Lowlands and, on occasion, towards England.

The Highland clans spoke a different language, Gaelic, whereas the language of Lowland Scotland and the court was Scots and in more modern times, English.

Highlanders dressed differently, had different

customs, and their wild mountain land sometimes seemed almost foreign to people living in the Lowlands.

It must be emphasised that Gaelic culture was very rich and story-telling, poetry, piping, the clarsach (harp) and other music all flourished and were greatly respected.

Highland culture was different from other parts of Scotland but it was not inferior or less sophisticated.

Central Government, whether in London or Edinburgh, sometimes saw the Gaelic clans as a challenge to their authority and some sent expeditions into the Highlands and west to crush the power of the Lords of the Isles.

Nevertheless, when the eighteenth century Jacobite Risings came along the cause of the Stuarts was mainly supported by Highland clans.

The word Jacobite comes from the Latin for James - Jacobus. The Jacobites wanted to restore the exiled Stuarts to the throne of Britain.

The monarchies of Scotland and England became one in 1603 when King James VI of Scotland (1st of England) gained the English throne after Queen Elizabeth died.

The Union of Parliaments of Scotland and England, the Treaty of Union, took place in 1707.

Some Highland clans, of course, and Lowland families opposed the Jacobites and supported the incoming Hanoverians.

After the Jacobite cause finally went down at Culloden in 1746 a kind of ethnic cleansing took place. The power of the chiefs was curtailed. Tartan and the pipes were banned in law.

Many emigrated, some because they wanted to, some because they were evicted by force. In addition, many Highlanders left for the cities of the south to seek work.

Many of the clan lands became home to sheep and deer shooting estates.

But the warlike traditions of the clans and the great Lowland and Border families lived on, with their descendants fighting bravely for freedom in two world wars.

Remember the men from whence you came, says the Gaelic proverb, and to that could be added the role of many heroic women.

The spirit of the clan, of having roots, whether Highland or Lowland, means much to thousands of people.

*Clan warfare produced a society where courage
and tenacity were greatly admired*

Chapter two:

In freedom's cause

A name of Scottish origin, Aitken and its numerous spelling variations is derived from what from medieval times has been the popular forename Adam, the Biblical figure whose name, in turn, is derived from the Hebrew 'adama', meaning 'earth'.

Now found all over Scotland, the name first made its appearance in the Berwickshire area of the Borders and in Lanarkshire, where there was a barony known as Akyne.

As early as 1384, there is a record of a Johannes Ade – a now redundant form of the Aitken name – in North Berwick, and of a John Atkynson in the same area in 1387.

The Aitken link with Berwickshire is particularly intriguing, in that it may go some way towards explaining how, along with bearers of names that include Craig, Cullen, Gardiner, Laing and Todd, they are recognised today as a sept, or sub-branch, of the distinguished Clan Gordon.

Although they came to be recognised as one

of the great clans of the northeast of Scotland, Clan Gordon, also known as the House of Gordon, had, in common with the Aitkens, an early origin in Berwickshire.

It is here that they are though to have taken their name from 'gor-dun', indicating a hill fort.

As a sept of Clan Gordon, the Aitkens are entitled to wear their clan tartan and share in their proud motto of 'Byland' ('Remaining') and crest of a stag's head atop a crown coronet, although they have their own proud motto of 'Strength and vigilance' and crest of an oak tree.

But this honour came at high cost, as many Aitkens shared in not only the Gordons' great fortunes, but also in their tragic misfortunes.

The Gordons and their kinsfolk such as the Aitkens were at the forefront of some of the most decisive episodes in Scotland's turbulent history.

This was not least during the Wars of Independence against its powerful southern neighbour, England, when they were stalwart in their support for the freedom fighter William Wallace and, later, the great warrior king Robert the Bruce, victor of the battle of Bannockburn in 1314.

It was through his support for Bruce that

Sir Adam Gordon was rewarded with the lordship of Strathbogie and Badenoch in the northeast of Scotland, far removed from the original Gordon and Aitken territory of Berwickshire.

It was in this new territory that the powerful Gordons became known as 'the Cock o' the North'.

Bruce also honoured Sir Adam by appointing him Scottish ambassador to the Papacy, and it was he, in 1320, who personally delivered to the Pope that rousing declaration of the nation's right to freedom and independence known as the Declaration of Arbroath.

In July of 1333, Sir Adam, along with many of his clan and kinsfolk such as the Aitkens, was killed at the disastrous battle of Halidon Hill, northwest of Berwick, when an invading English army inflicted a resounding defeat on a Scots force led by Archibald, Lord of Douglas.

Fifty-five years later, in August of 1388, the Gordon clan chief Sir John Gordon was killed at the battle of Otterburn, in Redesdale, Northumberland – a battle that nevertheless resulted in an English defeat.

In 1513, by which time the Gordons had been granted the Earldom of Huntly, Alexander Gordon, 3rd Earl of Huntly, was among the thousands of Scots killed at the battle of Flodden.

In the seventeenth century, bearers of the Aitken name, particularly in the Lowlands, were among those embroiled in the bitter and bloody war that raged between Crown and Covenant.

A National Covenant, pledging defence of the Presbyterian religion, had been signed in the Greyfriars Kirk, in Edinburgh, in February of 1638.

Copies were circulated throughout Scotland, and the hundreds of ordinary men and women who subscribed to it became known as Covenanters.

Following the restoration to the throne of Charles II in 1660, the death knell for the Covenanting movement was sounded when a Recissory Act was passed, declaring the Covenant illegal.

Episcopal rule was foisted on the Scottish Church, and all ministers who refused to adhere to this new order were deprived of their parishes.

Along with their congregations, many ministers literally took to the hills, preaching at open-air meetings known as conventicles.

Lookouts were posted to keep a wary eye out for the approach of Government troops, and justice was executed on the spot for those unfortunate enough to fall into their hands.

Constantly persecuted by the forces of

authority, the Covenanters rose in futile rebellion in November of 1666 and, as a sign of the harsh treatment that was to be subsequently meted out to them, many of the prisoners taken were tortured and hanged.

A Covenanting victory followed at the battle of Drumclog in June of 1679, only to be followed a few short weeks later by resounding defeat at the battle of Bothwell Brig, near Hamilton, by a force commanded by the Duke of Monmouth.

Nearly 800 Covenanters were killed and 1,400 taken prisoner. Many were imprisoned on the Bass Rock.

In September of 1683, George Aitken was one of three Covenanters taken prisoner after Bothwell Brig, who was involved in a daring moonlit escape from the confines of the Canongate tollbooth in Edinburgh.

They made use of a file that had been smuggled in to painstakingly saw through the bars of a window, drop to the street below, and make good their escape.

Chapter three:

Publishing and politics

Far from the fields of conflict, bearers of the Aitken name have made their mark on history through a range of more peaceful pursuits.

In common with many Scots, William Aitken, who was also known as William Aitkin, forged a new life for himself far from his native land.

Born in Edinburgh in 1785, he immigrated with his family to Canada as a young boy, later settling, at the age of 17, in the region of the Upper Mississippi, in America, where he found employment as a trader in a wide range of essential everyday goods.

By 1838 he had set himself up as an independent trader, operating a thriving trading post in Morrison County, Minnesota.

Known to have had at least two wives and at least 25 children, he died in 1851.

Aitken County in Minnesota and the city of Aitkin, also in Minnesota, are named in his honour.

Another Scottish bearer of the Aitken name to have found fame in North America was John Aitken, born in 1745 in Dalkeith, Midlothian.

Arriving in Philadelphia in 1771, he was apprenticed for a time to a goldsmith before, in 1787, branching out in a totally different direction as a music publisher.

For a time the only publisher of sheet music in the United States and, along with fellow Scot Alexander Reinagles, publisher of what was the hugely popular *A Selection of the Most Favorite Scots Tunes*, he was also the first in the United States to use the 'punch' engraving process for sheet music; he died in 1831.

Also born in Dalkeith, fourteen years before the birth of John Aitken and, it is reasonable to assume, one of his relations, Robert Aitken was the printer and publisher recognised for having published the first English language Bible in what was then the newly formed United States.

Emigrating from Scotland and establishing himself in Philadelphia as a bookseller in 1769, he became aware of how the War of Independence with Britain had cut off supplies of the Bible to North America.

Accordingly, he printed 10,000 Bibles, but this proved a commercial failure, with Aitken incurring a substantial financial loss.

A later initiative authorised by the Continental Congress for it to buy the Bibles and give them to discharged soldiers proved too late to recoup Aitken's losses; he died in 1802.

The progenitor of a particularly notable dynasty of bearers of the Aitken name, William Maxwell Aitken was the highly colourful and influential Canadian-British newspaper publisher better known as Sir Max Aitken, 1st Baron Beaverbrook.

Born in 1879 in Maple, Ontario, the son of a Scots-born Presbyterian minister, and moving at the age of one to Newcastle, Miramichi, New Brunswick, he is reputedly to have been aged only 13 when he first published his own, local, newspaper.

This proved to be a portent of great things to come in the newspaper world.

Scorning a formal higher education, he attended the University of New Brunswick for only a very brief period, before working for a time as an office boy in the law office of future Canadian Prime Minister Richard Bedford Bennet, then moving to Halifax, Nova Scotia.

It was here, while working for the businessman John F. Stairs, that he learned the basics of finance and business.

A quick learner, by 1904 he was general manager and a shareholder in Stairs's Royal Securities Corporation.

Acquiring control of the company following the death of Stairs, by 1910 the future newspaper magnate had acquired a monopoly in Canada Cement.

Alleged irregularities in stock transfers, however – irregularities that could have led to him being charged with securities fraud – saw him selling his shares in the company and quitting his native Canada for Britain.

Building what would become the newspaper publishing empire Beaverbrook Newspapers, firstly through the purchase of the *London Evening Standard*, what was then the ailing *Daily Express* in 1916 and later through founding the *Sunday Express*, he was also knighted and later granted a peerage as 1st Baron Beaverbrook.

'Beaverbrook' was the name of a small community near his boyhood home of Miramichi.

Holding the honorary rank of colonel in the Canadian Army during the First World War, establishing the Canadian War Memorials Fund and serving for a time as Britain's first Minister of Information, he also made a significant contribution to the Allied war effort during the Second World War.

This was through his appointment as Minister of Aircraft Production and, later, Minister of Supply.

Of his contribution, Britain's wartime leader Winston Churchill said of him: "His personal force and genius made this Aitken's finest hour."

After the end of the war, the *Daily Express* became the largest selling newspaper in the world, giving Beaverbrook immense influence over political issues of the day.

Of his shrewd business acumen, the writer H.G. Wells famously said of him: "If Max ever gets to Heaven, he won't last long.

"He will be chucked out for trying to pull off a merger between Heaven and Hell after having secured a controlling interest in key subsidiary companies in both places, of course."

The press baron died in 1964, and his ashes deposited in the town square of Miramichi, while the University of New Brunswick, of which he served for a time as Chancellor, has been a major benefactor of his charitable largesse.

Many other institutions and projects benefit to this day from the Beaverbrook Foundation.

Beaverbrook had been married for 21 years to Gladys Drury, until her death in 1927, and one of their three children was the Second World War fighter pilot, newspaper publisher and British Conservative party politician Sir Max Aitken.

Born in Montreal in 1910, he served with the RAF from 1935 to 1946 and was awarded both the Distinguished Flying Cross and the Distinguished Service Order.

He succeeded to his father's title following his death – but refused to adopt the title, stating that he wished there to be only one Lord Beaverbrook in his lifetime.

Following his death in 1985, after having served as chairman of Beaverbrook Newspapers, his son, the politician Max Aitken, born in 1951, assumed the title of 3rd Baron Beaverbrook

Yet another prominent member of the dynasty was Sir William Aitken, born in Nova Scotia in 1905 and a nephew of the 1st Baron Beaverbrook.

An RAF pilot during the Second World War and later a journalist and politician, he died in 1964.

Married to the late English socialite Penelope Aitken, a daughter of the 1st Baron Rugby, one of his children is the disgraced former British Conservative

Party politician Jonathan Aitken, who was born in 1942 in Dublin.

A war correspondent with the *London Evening Standard* during the 1960s, he later held a number of top government posts that included Minister of State for Defence Procurement and Chief Secretary to the Treasury.

Found guilty of perjury in 1999 after he had raised a libel action against the *Guardian* newspaper following its claims that he had violated ministerial rules by allowing an Arab businessman to pay for his stay in a Paris hotel, he received an 18-month prison sentence.

Chapter four:

On the world stage

Yet another member of the prominent Aitken dynasty founded by the 1st Baron Beaverbrook, but someone who pursues a career far removed from newspaper publishing and politics is his great granddaughter Maria Aitken.

Born in Dublin in 1945, the daughter of Sir William Aitken and sister of the former British government minister Jonathan Aitken, the actress, writer and film producer is best known for film roles that include the 1988 comedy *A Fish Called Wanda* and the 1998 *Jinnah*.

Through her first marriage to the English actor Nigel Davenport, she is the mother of the actor Jack Davenport. Now married to the novelist Patrick McGrath, she starred in the 1995 film adaptation of his novel *The Grotesque*.

From acting to broadcasting, **Kate Aitken** was a distinguished Canadian journalist and radio and television presenter.

Better known to her listeners and viewers as "Mrs A", she was born Kate May Scott in Beeton,

Ontario, in 1891, and took the Aitken name after marrying the businessman Henry Aitken.

One of the most prominent figures in the Canadian Broadcasting Corporation (CBC) throughout the 1930's, 40's and 50's, she presented a diverse range of shows that included topics such as cooking and etiquette and documentary journalism.

Serving on CBC's board of directors following her retirement as a presenter in 1957, she died in 1971.

In the world of contemporary music, **Matthew Aitken**, born in Coventry in 1956, is the British songwriter and record producer best known as one of the members of the popular music production trio Stock, Aitken Waterman, also known as SAW.

Made up of Aitken, Mike Stock and Pete Waterman, the trio enjoyed huge success throughout the 1980s writing and producing top hits that include Mel and Kim's 1987 *Respectable*, Rick Astley's 1987 *Never Gonna Give You Up*, and Australian star Kylie Minogue's 1989 *Hand on Your Heart*.

Born in Cuba in 1927 of mixed Cuban and Jamaican descent, Lorenzo Aitken, better known as **Laurel Aitken**, was the singer recognised today as 'The Godfather' of the Jamaican musical genre known as ska.

Settling with his family in Jamaica when he was 10-years-old, he went on to pioneer the ska form, while his 1958 hit single, *Little Sheila*, was the first Jamaican popular music record to be released in the United Kingdom. Responsible for hit albums that include his 1965 *Ska with Laurel* and, from 1989, *It's Too Late*, he died in 2005.

In a different musical genre, **Robert Aitken** is the contemporary Canadian composer and flautist who was born in 1939 in Kentville, Nova Scotia.

Becoming at the age of 19 the youngest principal flautist in the history of the Vancouver Symphony Orchestra, he went on to become a soloist with major symphony orchestras throughout the world.

Made a Member of the Order of Canada in 1993, he was also the recipient in 2003 of a Lifetime Achievement award from Canada's National Flute Association.

In contemporary pop music, **Hayley Aitken**, born in 1986 in Melbourne, is the Australian singer and songwriter whose hit singles include her 2001 *That Girl* and the 2002 *I Hate the Way I Love You*.

From music to the equally creative world of the written word, **Edward Aitken**, born in 1851 in Satara, India, where his father served as a missionary for the Free Church of Scotland, was the civil servant much better known for his humorous writings on India's natural history.

Also known to Anglo-Indian readers by his pen-name of Eha, and a founding member of the Bombay Natural History Society, his many popular writings include his 1883 *An Indian Naturalist's Foreign Policy* and, published nine years before his death in 1909 in his father's native Edinburgh, *The Common Birds of Bombay*.

Born in 1945 in Bath, **Jacqueline Aitken** is the best-selling British children's author who is published under her married name of Jacqueline Wilson.

Best known for her *Tracy Beaker* character and television adaptations of the tales in which she features, the author is the recipient of a number of awards that include Dame Commander of the Order of the British Empire (DBE), while from 2005 to 2007 she was the United Kingdom's Children's Laureate.

Born in 1793 in Camelon, Stirlingshire, **John Aitken** was the noted Scottish journalist and bookseller who, before his death in 1833, helped to found the *Edinburgh Literary Journal*, while Adam Aitken, better known as **Jack Aitken**, was a distinguished Scottish lexicographer.

Born in Edinburgh in 1921, he served with the Royal Artillery during the Second World War before re-commencing his studies at Edinburgh University into the origins of the Scottish and Celtic languages. Collaborating with the equally distinguished Sir William Craigie, he helped to compile the *Scottish National Dictionary* and the *Dictionary of the Older Scottish Tongue*, taking over control of the lengthy project on Craigie's death.

It was not until 2000, two years after his death, that the dictionaries – available now under the collective title of the *Dictionary of the Scots Language* – were finally completed and dedicated to him in his honour.

On the field of battle, **Robert Aitken**, born in 1828 in Cupar, Fife was a Scottish recipient of the Victoria Cross (VC), the highest award for bravery in the face of enemy action for British and Commonwealth forces.

He had been a lieutenant in the 13th, Bengal Native Infantry, during the Bengal Mutiny, when, during the defence of the Lucknow Residency in 1857, he carried out a number of actions that included attacking and capturing two enemy guns.

Later promoted to the rank of colonel, he

died in 1887, while his VC is now on display in the National Army Museum in Chelsea.

Bearers of the Aitken name have also excelled, and continue to excel, in the highly competitive world of sport.

On the fields of European football, **Roy Aitken**, born in 1958 in Irvine, Ayrshire, is the former Scottish defender who played for teams that include Celtic, where he was nicknamed "The Bear", and who won 57 caps playing for the Scottish national team between 1980 and 1991. Now an equally successful coach for teams that have included Birmingham City and Dubai club Al-Ahli, he also managed Scottish Premier League club Aberdeen from 1995 to 1997.

Born in Peterhead in 1894, **Willie Aitken**, also known as Billy Aitken, was the Scottish football forward who, throughout a long career, played for teams that include Rangers, Newcastle United and, from 1929 to 1930, Italian club Juventus, in addition to managing a number of foreign clubs; he died in 1973.

Also on the football field, **Charlie Aitken**, born in 1942, and from Gorebridge, Midlothian, is the former defender who, at the time of writing, holds the record for appearances with English club Aston Villa – having played for them between August of 1959 and

May of 1976. Before his retirement from the game, he also played for a time in the United States for the New York Cosmos.

From football to the equally popular game of ice hockey, **Jonathan Aitken** is the retired Canadian defenceman, born in 1978 in Edmonton, Alberta, who between 1998 and 2007 played for teams that include the Boston Bruins and the Chicago Blackhawks.

Born in 1967 in Scarborough, Ontario, **Brad Aitken** is the former ice hockey left wing who played for teams that include the Pittsburgh Penguins and the Edmonton Oilers.

In the cerebral world of chess, **James Aitken**, born in 1908 in Calderbank, Lanarkshire was Scottish chess champion on no less than ten occasions between 1935 and 1965. Aitken, who was engaged in highly secretive work during the Second World War at Bletchley Park, Buckinghamshire, in the breaking of the codes of the German military's Enigma machines, also represented Scotland in four Chess Olympiads before his death in 1983.

Recognised as having been one of New Zealand's greatest mathematicians and the subject of a biography sub-titled *The Human Computer*, **Alexander Aitken** was born in 1895.

Noted during his lifetime for his prodigious memory and ability to carry out complex mental calculations, he studied for his doctorate in mathematics at Edinburgh University, where in 1925 he was appointed to a research and teaching position.

Elected to the Royal Society of Edinburgh in the same year and to the Royal Society of London eleven years later for his work in algebra, statistics and numerical analysis, he also wrote a memoir of his First World Experiences, *Gallipoli to the Somme: Recollections of a New Zealand Infantryman*.

An accomplished musician in addition to mathematician, he died in 1967, while an annual Aitken Prize is awarded in his honour by the New Zealand Mathematical Society.

In the world of art, **Robert Ingersoll Aitken**, born in San Francisco in 1878 and who died in 1949, was the American sculptor whose most noted work is the West pediment of the United States Supreme Court building in Washington, with its inscription of *Equal Justice Under Law*.

In the often cut-throat world of politics, **David Aitken**, born in 1853 in Flint Township, Michigan, and who died in 1930, was the American Republican politician who served as a U.S.

Representative for Michigan from 1893 to 1897, while, in New Zealand, **James Aitken**, born in 1849 and who died in 1921, served as Mayor of Wellington from 1900 to 1904.

In Scottish politics, **Bill Aitken**, born in Glasgow in 1947, is the Conservative politician who, in addition to having served as a Glasgow City councillor, also served for a time in the Scottish Parliament as his party's spokesperson on justice and as convener of the Parliament's justice committee.

Taking to the heavens, **Robert Grant Aitken** was the distinguished American astronomer who was born in 1864 in Jackson, California.

Particularly noted for his study and cataloguing of double stars and working from California's Lick Observatory, his numerous awards include the 1932 Gold Medal of the Astronomical Society, while Asteroid 3070 Aitken is named in his honour in addition to the impact crater, Aitken, on the far side of the Moon.

The astronomer, who died in 1951, was the grandfather of the Zen Buddhist teacher and writer **Robert Baker Aitken**. Born in 1917 in Philadelphia, Aitken, a Zen Buddhism teacher in what is known as the Harada-Yasutani lineage, founded a Zen Buddhist centre in Honolulu in 1959 along with his wife, **Anne**

Hopkins Aitken, who was born in 1911 in Cook County, Illinois. He died in 2010, six years after the death of his wife.

One particularly colourful and infamous bearer of the Aitken name was James Aitken, born in Edinburgh in 1752 and who, because of the artistic ambitions and pretensions he harboured, is better known to posterity as **John the Painter**.

Ironically, however, it is not as an artist that he is best known, but as what one biography describes as "the first modern terrorist."

In a short and varied career that embraced shoplifting and highway robbery, he spent some time in America and returned to Britain in 1775 imbued with revolutionary ideals. Launching a one-man crusade against the might of the British Crown in general and the Royal Navy in particular, he carried out a series of arson attacks over a period of several months on naval facilities in Bristol and Portsmouth.

Eventually tracked down and brought to justice, he gained the highly dubious distinction in March of 1777 of being hanged from the mizzenmast of a ship in Portsmouth dockyard – the highest gallows used in an English execution – watched by an estimated crowd of 20,000.